Olivia Rose

Soul Purpose

A book of Poems

Cover Illustration

by Whitecap Productions

Liquid Cat

PUBLISHING ®

Soul Purpose

Liquid Cat Publishing House
A Division of Liquid Cat Universal
Los Angeles, California

ISBN: 9798413731765

This book is dedicated to those who believed in me when I didn't believe in myself.

Prologue

I hope this book gives you the courage to find your own path and be who you were always destined to be. This book is full of raw emotions. I created it as a safe space for you to feel your own raw emotions. I hope in reading this book, you will start a journey to find your soul's purpose. Write with love.

SOUL'S CONTENTS

Soul Purpose Intro

*I have created something
From scratch.*

*With every fiber in my
Being.*

*Every tear that was
Shed.*

*Every smile I ever had.
Made with*

*Love.
Care.
Compassion.*

A Bakery.

This is my Soul's Purpose.

*I hope this inspires you to find
Your spark.*

*I hope this inspires you to find
Your Soul's Purpose.*

Blessed Be.

R.O.O.T

Rewrite

Our

Own

Truths

Drum Circle

Gathered in a circle,
Each with a drum
Playing along
One by one
Song by song
Beat by beat.
Allowing the music
To coarse through our veins
Red blood cells, pumping

                            To our hearts
                                 Lub, dub
                    Pushing, back out
                                    Blood.
            Delivering to the rest
                      Of our bodies.
            Each strike of the drum
                Catches the attention
      Of the hairs on the back of our necks
          As they stand at attention
        Sending chills down our spines
         As we bellow to the sounds
                      Of the drum.
                   Fire, soaring.

Roaring.
Wildly, dancing to the beat
Of the drums.
The sway of her hips
Cut through the air
Like glass.
Swift, sensual, sexy.
Reclaiming her power
Right before our eyes.
We watched her
In amazement, awe

                                  A trance

Hypnotized.
We fell under her spell.
Seduced us.
Until we became one,
With the drums.
Kundalini.
Echoes nourishing our souls.
Coursing through our veins,
Swaying our hips.
Beat by beat
Song by song
One by one.
Dance, as one
Kundalini.

Cycles

Laying in a pool of blood
I was not expecting you this early
Arriving, unannounced.
You did knock,
More of a bang,
On the walls of my uterus.

As I lay cramping
Groaning,
In agony.

Now I know,
I should not complain.
You showing up is a beautiful thing.
You are the essence of life.

You flow through my body.
Everyday.
So what makes this so different?

You're getting the room ready,
Comfortable.
When the time comes
For one to move in.

Half him.
Half me.
That will bake in this oven of mine.

Until then,
It is the same cycle.
Time to shed the old
Bring in the new.

We will create this space together,
Body,

Where we will have a roommate,
9 months.

Someone who will make me
A Mother.
A lover,
Of the little things

Life has to offer.
But until then,
It is the same cycle.
Time to shed the old
To bring in the new.

Brown Sugar

Brown sugar skin,
White sugar mixed with cinnamon

Blended, to make you.
Soft, silky skin,

Eyes, pools of honey
Harvested, from

Beehives.
Hair, texture of clouds,

Beautiful, black, bouncy locks.
Curves, like the back roads in the mountains.

A smile, like a loaded gun,
Ready to pull the trigger.

At any moment.

Explosion

Full of rage.
Anger.
Seeing red. Bright blood red.
Ironic, I'm bleeding on this
Full Moon.

Blood Full Moon.
Some days,
Anger, rage take over
My body.
Build-up.
Like the air in a balloon.
But I have to pretend, I'm okay.
When I want to burst.
Pressure increases.

POP!

Erupting like a volcano
Whose lava has no place to go,
Without hurting,
Burning.
Those around me.
Those I love.

Growing Pains

Sometimes, well most times
I feel like I'm losing my mind
Am I?
I see differently.

Sometimes, well most times
I feel like I'm losing my mind
Am I?
Perspectives.

Is this growth?
Coming from the murky waters
From the dark depths of
Despair?

Loneliness?
Becoming something, someone
I never thought I would
Be.

Growth.

Transformation.

Sometimes, well most times
I feel like I'm losing my mind.
Am I?
Who is this person?

That I have become?
Do I know you?
Have we met
Whose skin is this?

It's not mine.
There were cracks.

Bruises.
Scars.

Full of hurt.
Dark thoughts.
Depression.
Where have these flowers come from?

My tears, did they water you?
Did they help you?
Bloom?
Flourish?

Was it painful?
Being broken?
Having to tend your own garden?
Weeding yourself of the hurt?

Of the dead dirt?
Was it hard to start over?
Having to replant your own seeds?
To nurture your own needs?

Sometimes, well most times
I feel like I'm losing my mind
I am not.
This is growth.

Indomitable Fear

How dare you,
                    Allow me,
My Goddess
            To live in this constant state,
An indomitable spirit
                    Of emotional whirlwind?
Driven by traumas.
                    Hurt.

Disappointment.
Anxiety.

                                    Yet, she is the one,
                                    Who defies all odds.

How dare you,
Take the wheel
Of my emotions and steer
Them towards the cliff

                                        Where we hang?
                            She, who births life.
                            As we teeter totter.
                                    Back and forth.

Unbeknownst of what could happen.
        To me.
                    To you.

To us.
She who takes life.
How dare you believe
You are innocent.
When I can prove you guilty.

Of your beauty.
        Of your chaos.

                                    How dare you
                              Be the death of me.
                         An adventure I sought
                              Wrapped in one.
                                  How dare you.
                              Fear yourself?

YOU.
Are an indomitable spirit.
You are in control.
top living in the
State of Fear.

A Letter to You, Wherever You Are

Why didn't they warn me
That it would hurt this bad?
When you left.
I wasn't prepared for all of the emotions.

That I have.
That I had.
No call.
No text.

Just like that.

Gone.

No goodbye.
No "I'll see you later"

Nothing.

My heart breaks every time I think of you
and
a lump in my throat forms.
Here comes the breakdown.

Who knew that losing you would suck.
I had
so many plans for us.
But now they are gone.
Vanished. Into thin air.

Magic trick.

Nonexistent. Now tell me.
Where did you go? Are you happy?
Do you miss me?

The phone calls and pictures. The laughs and the teardrops.

Sometimes, I look back.
But I try not to stay there,
Too long.

How are you?
Is all I want to ask you.
Give you a hug
is all I want to do.

I guess you're a question that will never
Be answered.
I guess that's something I'll
Have to live with, too.

Anyways,
I hope you're doing well.

Wherever you are.

Kisses from the Rain

You're back.
I missed you.
I love when you visit.
You bring back memories,
Of places that I long to go back to.
Of places I have yet been.
Something familiar,
Home.
The way you wake me,
Lightly tapping against my window.
Like pebbles being tossed to get my attention.
Notifying me,
That you have made your way back.
To me.
After being gone
For some time.
When I go outside to greet you,
Your kisses gently
Graze my cheeks.
Forehead.
Nose.
Ever so slightly.
Chills explore the nerves around my spine.
Every time I feel your presence.
I have longed for home, alongside you.

Endless Thinking

A never-ending void

Of thoughts

In my mind

Spiraling staircase

That keeps on going.

And going.

And going.

Make it stop.

I gotta get off.

Strangers

One moment
     You are strangers.

The next,
     You know everything
About each other.

Finally,
     You are strangers
Again.

Mourning a Loss

What hurts worse?
A lost friendship or
A breakup?

    I don't know
    They both know everything
    About you.
    Yet, they have to pretend
    Like they don't
    When things come to an
    End.

So you tell me.

Either way,
The Heart mourns

Arrival

What is this feeling?
Tears of joy?
Sorrow?

Not bringing you into this world,
Just yet.

I constantly think
About you.
The moment you will
Arrive.

I long to hold you.
To love, you,
Unconditionally.

Mixed emotions fill my head.

But until then.

I will think about you.
I will wait for your arrival.

To finally come home.

To us.

I love you.

Already.

Sky Fires

Sacral Chakra
You shine bright,

Orange.
Like the sunrise.

Sunset.
Setting the sky,

On fire.
Burning,

With passion.

Wholehearted Love

```
I fear that you'll wake up one day.
And find it all unattractive.
I fear my flaws will make you,
        Flee.

But,

When I look into your eyes.
They remind me

        I am loved.
```

DawnBreaker

I have dreamt of this,
My whole life.
Waking up next to you
On a Sunday morning.

The rain, knocking on the window.
Begging, to come in.
To join us.
The touch of your hands on my body
Following the curves,

That match those of mountains.
The dips, valleys, hills.
You have it mapped out.
As if you have traveled this area before.

Your touch feels familiar.
You feel like home.
Brushing your lips against mine.
Sends signals racing down my spine.

My hairs stand at attention.
Waiting, for you to continue,
Your journey down the mountain.

My body
Gazing into your eyes
As they change color.

Bluer than the ocean.
Greener than the grass.
Gray on rainy days, like today.
You scan me, Taking in every detail.

Every inch
Of my body.

I get self-conscious.
You will spot something,
That you won't like.
My imperfections.

Bruises. Scars. Cuts.

The harm.
That the world threw at me.

The harm.
That I inflicted upon
Myself.

I fear that you will find it

Unattractive.
Repulsive.
Unflattering.

I fear my flaws will make you abandon
The journey.

But you remind me,
That you love adventures.

It All Hurts

Who knew that pain could come
From someone
So close
To you.

An idea of you.
An image they cannot release.
A past you.
Who no longer exists.

The person you used to be
The person you worked so hard
To change.

To love, fully.
The past you

Was hurt.
Shamed.
Guilty.
Angry.

The past you
Was constantly in Defense mode.
Guarded. Wounded like a caught dog.

An elephant pierced by a spear,
          Straight to the heart.

<u>HEART</u>

Heal
Everything

And
Remember, it does take
Time.

Sharp Tongue

The words that you
Spit
Knives piercing my body.

Straight through
The Heart.
No remorse, you had.
As you watched me bleed out.

I forgave you.
Without an apology.
You chewed it up
And spit it back
In my face.
As I lay here, bleeding out.

Vulnerable.
You tied me
To the back of your car.
Dragged me through the mud.
Spat on me
With your venomous tongue.

Slashed my face.
Left.
Right.
You left me.
For dead.
Here I lay.

Fighting with myself.
Should I pick up my pieces?
Or lay here?

And feel bad for myself?

Fuck that.
I'll take your venom.

And use it to my advantage
To recreate myself.

Again.

Sibling Rivalry

One-on-one
A versus battle.
Super Smash Bros. Brawl
A racing match.
This isn't a video game.
It's a real life battle.
That is tearing this family
Apart.

I'll forfeit
Let you win.
Victory tastes sweet.
Doesn't it?

I'm tired of fighting.
I'm removing myself.
Player 2, are you sure you want to
Exit the game?
Yes.

GAME OVER!

Mirror, Mirror on the Wall, Reflection is All

We are all mirrors of ourselves. As I sit here and watch. How you treat those who love you, with anger; I saw myself in you. A hurt soul. Lost. Confused. Angry. Frustrated. Pain. Guilt. Shame. You are trying to mask it. The best way you can. But I see you. You are cracking. I, too, was there. Experiencing the same feelings. Same emotions.The constant substance abuse. Going out. Lashing out. Hurting those I love.
You, too,
have hurt those
That you love.

Mirror, Mirror on the wall...
Have I grown and changed at all?

Yes, you have. I see you in me. This is a lesson. This is a reflection. Of the past. The work that has been begun. And continues. The healing is linear. A rollercoaster. Of emotions. Healing, nurturing the wounds. I see you in me. Reacting before thinking. Letting the feelings take over. The defense mode. I can guide you. But I guess you have to experience your own darkness. Before you see the light.
Before you see
your own light
as Your potential.

Mirror, Mirror on the wall...
Was this a test to see if I would fall
Back into old habits? Did I pass? Did I Fail?

I do not know. Only time will tell. But I know
that this allowed for reflection on how far you
have come. How much you have changed. How much
you have grown. I hope what you are going through
on your journey. Makes you realize who you are.
Pause. Reflect. Appreciate. All that you have
been through.
I hope you realize. It is okay to feel.
But do not forget.
To heal.

Mirror, Mirror on the wall…
Am I a reflection for all
to know that one can change?

You can't save everyone.
But you saved yourself.
From being submerged into the depths
Of darkness.
I hope you are able to swim to the surface.
To save yourself,
Before it's too late.

Mirror, Mirror on the wall…
Thank you for the reflection.
Thank you for the wake up call.

Gratitude to Gaia

I came back home to you,
        Mother Gaia,
Away from the bright lights.
Of the big cities.

                        That have chiseled away
                            At your beauty.
                    Replacing parts of you with
                Buildings, factories, businesses.

I came back home to you,
        Mother Gaia,
To your roots
Where you exposed them

                    Knowing you're safe from any harm.

I came back home to you,
        Mother Gaia,
To explore your curves
To become one with your rivers

                            To exchange energies.

I came back home to you,
        Mother Gaia,
To ponder, in your beauty.
Gawking at the natural wonders.

                            Of your world.
                    Here in this forest.

Your vulnerability leaves me
Breathless.
As your tears fall from the sky.

Who hurt you?

I want to ask.
How can I make you feel better?
I came back home to you,
     Mother Gaia,
Because I wanted to understand
You.

                          On a soul level.
            The animals that call you home.
                And feel safe in your arms.
            The beauty that you have birthed
                              For years.

I came back home to you,
     Mother Gaia,
Because I wanted to be
Closer to you.

                     Without distractions.

                     To bask in your sun.

                To bathe in your moonlight.

I came back home to you,
     Mother Gaia,
To rest and recharge
In the safety of your arms.

               To remind myself where I came from
                 To feel connected to you, again.
                            So that, we two,
                              Can be one.

Moon Manic

I whisper all my secrets
To you.
While you sit and listen.
Intensely, shining your
Light.
Down on me.

    Spotlight.
    Spoken words.
    Midnight sounds.

Secrets to the moon.

Golden Days

A warm hug
From the light that
Is expelled from you.
Bright energy.
Even on the darkest
Days.

     Solar Plexus.

Food for the soul,
Sun kissed.
Pure bliss.

Healing Cycle

Nurture.

Water.

Grow.

Repeat.

Story Telling

Don't rewrite old stories.
Create new ones.
You, too,
are a poet.

Swimming Pools

Your eyes are pools of
Honey.
That I could swim
In for the rest of my
Life.

Beautiful eyes change
Caramel covered sweet apples
Golden yellow, green.

Ocean Currents

I am water.
Always flowing
Ever changing.
Pushing, pulling.
Inhale, exhale.
Ebb, flow
Of the currents.

The moonlight dances
Upon the waves
Shimmering
Like the dew drops
On a quiet Sunday
Morning.
Glistening.

99 percent of the depths
Have yet to be discovered.
99 percent of me, I have yet
To uncover.
So much beauty she holds
Down below.
So much beauty she holds

On the surface.
I, too, hold that beauty.
Down below.
I, too, hold that beauty
On the surface.
Yet, there are secrets so deep
That we dare not speak

Grasp them tightly.

An octopus holding on
To a sunken ship.

Down below.
In her cave.
In my cave.

Buried treasure, hides.
In the depths.
For some things are not meant
To be discovered.
As the greed, for the need
To know what it holds

Will take away
From the beauty of the
Mystery.
I am you.
You are me.
We are one.
Water.

The ocean.
The rivers.
The creeks.
Ever changing
Pushing, pulling
Inhale, exhale
Ebb, flow.

I am water

Warrior Woman

My eyes, warm caramel. My skin. Honey golden.
Sun-kissed with freckles. Ten fingers. Nails
bitten. Anxiety ridden.

Ten toes. One nose, pierced. Two arms. Two
hands. One smile, so sweet. Thirty-two teeth
but one crooked, a smile that would generate
enough energy to light up rooms.

For over a million miles. A body full of art.
Scars. Scabs. Burns. Piercing. Tattoos. That all
makes me who I am

Who am I? Hair big, cloud like. Dreamy. Curly.
Like the leaves on trees. Bushes, lush and
beautiful. The curves of my body mimic the
country roads. Navigating up the mountain side.
Effortlessly. Carved out. A force to be reckoned
with. As I carry myself with Courage. Passion.
Determination. Fire. I am a fucking Aries.

I am the daughter of the women before me. Strong
roots. Like those of trees. Wild. Like the fires
burning in my soul. Emotional. Like the weather
that is ever changing. I am a Goddess. A fearless
Warrior. A powerful Woman.

Societal Block

Humans think too much.
We never know what to write
Or what is right.
But we are learning
Each and every day
That's okay
To not know.
That's what the pen is for
It'll do the talking for us.

As she glides across the beautiful
Acorn colored paper.
She knows what to say.
The way she moves, gracefully.
Elegant.
Smooth.
Without pause.
She knows what to say
For us.

And that is beautiful.
Magickal, really.

Humans think too much.
It kills the art and the magick.
The love, the fun, the spark.

This idea, that what we create
Has to be perfect.
A finished product.
Up to society's standards.
But not our own standards?
How does that make any sense?
Why do we allow our own egos
To dictate what we create?
Why do we allow others egos

To dictate what we make?
Stop thinking about what others say.
Stop thinking about their views.
Quit thinking, worrying

Take that pen
Paint brush
Marker
And leave a fucking mark.
An imprint.

On those who matter most.
Create art
For the beautiful
Magickal
Kind hearts of
This
World.

Stop thinking.

Create.

S.A.C.R.A.L

Sexual Desires

Are

Creative,

Raw,

And yet, these desires are

Looked down upon
        (and suppressed by society's standards)

LA

Los Angeles, California

Breathtaking sunny days
Dark and mysterious ways

Bright lights, big city

Yet, still lonely.

A Witch's Dream

I long for home.
Sitting by the window
Fog rolling in.

I long for home.
A cottage in the forest
Or by the sea
Isolated from the world
A place where I am safe
To be me.

I long for home.
A place where love resides
The fireplace is always going
A cauldron full of surprises
Where the magick happens.

I long for home.
Where animals greet me
Where the wind whispers to me
Her secrets of the forest
Of the sea
Where the ocean comes crashing,
Knocking at my door.
Begging to come in.

I long for home.
Where the sun sneaks in
Through the windows
Just to give me kisses
In the morning.
At 6am.
And kisses me again at 4pm.
Or 7pm.
Depending on when she felt
The need to go.

        I long for home.
Where the moon listens to my cries
My secrets.
My soul.
At 3am.
And tells me that she can't wait
To hear it all over, again.

        I long for home.
Where the kitchen is always full
Foods, spices, herbs, spells, and magick
Where the fae greet me as I gather
Water from the River
Where I gaze at my beauty
Alongside
        Oshun
        Yemaya
      Aphrodite
For hours.
Where the field of daisies invites me
To lay
Watching clouds float by
Making flower crowns.

        I long for home.
Where I can roam
Naked.
Wild.
Free.

        I long for home.

Divine Feminine

There you were emerging
From the ocean
Right before my eyes
Like the Goddess you are

White dress
Clinging to your body
Afraid to let go
Skin shining, sparkling

Water beads mimic those of diamonds
Dripping from your body.
As the sun's rays shine on them.
Tickling them,

Dancing on your body.
Your eyes gleaming
I can't look away from you.
Your hair compliments your face,

Washed by the ocean
Dripping in salt water
Glowing
An angel.

Gracefully walking towards me
I shouldn't be in the presence of this woman.
This Angel
This Goddess

A smile swims across her face.
She looks back at me
I stare back
Gawking

Soul searching, deep in her eyes.
I realize...

She is me.
I step into her power.

This is me.
I am the Divine Woman.
My highest self.

Bloodline

Root Chakra
Takes me back

To the past lives.
Ancestors

It's time to break
The generational

Curses.

Golden Compass

Solar Plexus
Show me the light
My intuition
Guide me down the path
Left or right?

Heart Chakra
Help me decide
What is it that gives me
Sparks in this life?

Throat Chakra
So many words in my
Head, that I can't get out
    Come on girl
     Spit it out.
SPEAK!

Third Eye Chakra
Eye see you
For who you are
Do you see you? For who you are?
Look beneath the surface.
It's deeper than that.

Crown Chakra
I am one whole
I have always been
It just took some time
To do soul
Searching.

Food is Love

Cucumbers are my favorite
I like the way you serve them
To me
On a platter
Makes me feel like I matter.

Every morning, I wake up
7 A.M. on the dot.
Just so I can go in
The kitchen and brew
You a hot pot
Of coffee.

Gratitude to Goddess

I heard your voice
     Down,
By the river.

I couldn't make out what
   You were saying
But I know it was
   You.

Talking to the
   Fae.
Singing the songs of the
   Spirits.
   Creatures.
   Critters.
That call this place
   Home.

Your water ran Cold.
Yet, so Enticing.
I felt Home.
Down there with You.

I know it was You.
Thank you for the visit
My Goddess. Blessed Be.
My Beautiful Queen. Oshun.

A Pet's Honor

I know that we can't communicate
But, just know that I see the demons
You face.

And I will do EVERYTHING
In my power
To protect you.

Every hour.
Whether we are cuddling together in bed
Or sitting on the couch

We are in this together.
My best friend, forever.
That, I can promise you.

Heartbreak Prison

There you were
Sitting in the bar, Cracking jokes
Being the life of the party.
Like you always used to.

The neon open sign, Blinking.
Winking at me.
Trying to seduce me,
To come in

For one drink. I can't,
Bare to look at you
To face you will break me.

I whisper to you
Goodbye.
But I know You'll never hear it
when I walk away from the window.

Out of the corner of my eye
I see you turn around
Like you just saw a spirit.
You touched the back of your neck
Your hairs rose.

At least now I know
I'm not the only one
Living in Heartbreak Prison.

Ancestor Answers

You come to me in my dreams
Subconscious.

      What message do you bring?

Ancestor, please.
How do I break this

Bloody curse that has
Been placed on me?

Grounded

Keep me grounded
Safe and stable.
   Muladhara
Like the roots of trees
Strong, durable.
   Muladhara
Let go of the fear.
Find yourself
   Muladhara
In the comfort of trust
Faith
Stability.
   Muladhara

Let this energy portal
Be free from stagnation
   Svadhisthana
The lack of creativity
Sexual Desire
   Svadhisthana
Burst with passion
Expression
Sensuality
   Svadhisthana

Shine bright like the sun
Golden Yellow
   Manipura
Warrior Spirit
Determination
Drive
   Manipura

Heart is open
Full of love
   Anahata
Compassion

                                   Appreciation
                                      Anahata
                                  Forgive others
                                  Accept yourself
                                      Anahata

The lump in the throat
Something I can't express
      Vishuddha
SPEAK!
What is your HIGHEST TRUTH?
      Vishuddha

                           What is it that you see?
                        Beyond this physical realm?
                                         Anja
                                        Expand
                           Beyond the 2 eyes
                                         Anja
                                         Look,
                     See what hides behind the veil.
                                         Anja

You have done it
Reached the top of the mountain
      Sahaswara
Enlightenment
Pure Connection
      Sahaswara
You are Whole.
      Sahaswara

Ponder

Bird on the wall
Curious and small
What goes through your mind?
Anything at all?

SOLAR PLEXUS

Somewhere inside of you, there's this

Optimistic

Light, that is waiting to

Appear in this world that is full of

Ruthlessness. Anger. Hurt.

Please

Let this light

Explore the world and fill it with more

Xenas, Warrior Princesses

Unique women, whose

Self-esteem will burn bright; Golden with
confidence

Tale of the Suburbs

I reside in the suburbs. Where it's sunny 365 days of the year. Where the sun rises at 6AM. Fog rolls in at 4PM. And clears just in time for the cotton candy skies at 7PM. Where the local surf kids know all the secret spots. Where the jocks are practicing for their sports. Academic kids are studying, day in. Day out.

The place where you can sit in the parking lots and still smell the sea salt air. Salty breezes. Sweeping over us. Where the Friday Night Lights of high school football games were all the rage. Where every kid knows where they are attending college. Who they want to be. And why. You know that song "Suburbs" by Arcade Fire? Well shit. They were right. The suburbs can definitely be a lonely drive. Even without a car.

Friends you thought were close, soon leave. And forget what you've gone through together. Lovers become ex's. A place that is supposed to feel like home feels more foreign. Strange. Was it really home to begin with? Yes, I participated in sports. Extra curricular activities. But that seemed to be the only common interest.

I knew I never belonged. But how the FUCK do you EXPRESS that at 18 years old? "You're overreacting." "You're dramatic" You have LOADS of friends.

       . . . Sure I do . . .
       ...But they don't know the real me.

Do you know what I have gone through in this fucked up town? Do you know what I've been through? Growing up in a place where your friends had both of their parents? And I only had one? A single black woman raising 5 kids. Alone. Maybe with the help of some. Constantly moving. Living in a 2 bedroom apartment with 6 people. Stressful, I know. Cars were repossessed. Fun stuff, I know.

Do you know what it felt like, being shy? And feeling like the only reason why people talked to me was because they felt bad? Do you know how much anger there is? How much pain, hurt, guilt? Fill my body. Fill my bones? Do you know how much heartache I carry with me? On a daily basis?

NO. YOU FUCKING DON'T.

You wanna know why? Because in this town, you mask that shit. Fuck all of that. In this town, once in high school…it becomes a competition. These parents make sure that their kids get into the top notch school. Top notch jobs. Go be a brown noser. These people are so fake, they will eat you alive while breaking bread with you. Right in front of your face. Friend or foe. Watch out. You never know who is going to backstab you.

WELCOME TO THE SUBURBS!

Forbidden Fruit

I take a bite of you
Juices, running down
The sides of my mouth
Pomegranate.

Escaping the waterfall of
My salivating tongue
They say that apples are
The forbidden fruit.
I beg to differ.

It's you.

SAVIOR

I am sorry.
I could not save you
From tying the noose
Around your neck.

I am sorry.
I could not save you
From dangling at the seams.
Of the ceiling

I am sorry.
I could not save you
From the pain that your heart
Held on to so tightly

I am sorry.
I could not save you
From the anger that resided
In your body

I am sorry.
I could not save you
While I was saving myself
From my anger.

I am sorry.
I could not save you
From the thoughts in your mind
That were living rent free

I am sorry.
I could not save you
I feel I have failed you.
Could you ever forgive me?

For leaving
To deal with

My own
Demons?
While you suffered.

    Silently.
    With yours?

I am sorry.
I could not save you
While you were drowning.
I'm supposed to protect you.

    But I have failed you.
    I am sorry.

Could you ever forgive me?

Ducks in a Row

I used to pick my brothers
Up from school.

One by one
Like a row of ducks.

1,2,3,4
Alright, everyone is here.

    I miss those days

Even if they weren't always
Filled with sunshine and cheers.

STICKY FINGERS

You took a bite of me.
    Sweet like a Georgia Peach

In the summertime.
    You got tired.

And with time,
    Switched fruit.

Watermelon will do.
    That's when I knew.

You found your favorite fruit.
    And we were through.

STICKY FINGERS, TOO

I am not innocent, either.
    I took a bite of you, Strawberry Sweet.

You were my favorite treat.
    At first; Then I grew bored.

Of the same sweetness; the same flavor.
    And switched.

From cherries, to pineapples.
    Even pomegranates.

 Many fruits, I could not decide.
    Yet, none of it satisfied me.

I was greedy.
    I, too, had sticky fingers.

The juices from me
    run

Down the side of my leg.
    Persephone's favorite.

It's that time, again.
    Where the seeds are being Expelled.

I'm RIPE, can't you see?
Pick me

THROAT

Truth will always be
Heard,

Regardless

Of what
Anyone will try to
Tell you.

WHAT A TRIP

Euphoria fills my body
When I take a dose of you.
I see clearly.
High Definition.
I feel the energy of the
Trees; their vibrations beneath
My feet.
Sending me signals.
As if I am
One of them.

On the flip side
Horror, fills my body
When I take a dose of you.
Looking at strangers faces
Turn into demons.
High definition.
I hear their thoughts.
Judgment.
Pain.
Hurt.
Fake.

I gotta get out here
It was bliss
Now it's a mess
WHAT A FUCKING TRIP

Cloud Nine

Standing outside the Nomad
39 degrees fahrenheit in the middle of February.
City snow stains the ground
With black muck.
Dirt and oil mixed with the purest form
Of water
Falling from the sky.
12 AM, whiskey dances with my
Taste buds on my tongue

ENCORE!
DANCE SOME MORE!

I light the end of the cigarette.
Smoke forms.
I take a drag.
The city looks bleak.
Sad.
Depressed, really.
Rundown by the violence that
Lives here.

I take another drag.
Exhaled smoke begins to form
An image that I am quite familiar with.
You.

Memories flood back to me.
An avalanche.
All at once.
The love that we made between the
Sheets in our one bedroom apartment.
In the inner city of a foreign place.
Where everyone was a stranger.
Except for us.

The walks we would take

Down to the local cafe.
Where we would have breakfast.
Sleepy Saturday mornings.
Arguments that we had
Echoed, down the halls
Knocking on our neighbors doors.

I took another drag.
Your image appears, again.
Our first date, at my favorite place.
Walks on the beach,
Homemade sushi; Banana pancakes
All my favorite foods to make me stay.
And I did.

Now we are here
Where the city snow stains the streets.
Slushy black, Dirt and oil mixed with the purest
form of water
Falling like angels from the sky.

I finished the cigarette,
And stumble back into the bar.
Where you are. You look up, smiling.
Your drink in hand while Billy is making mine.

I can't help but grin, and think
I know you're staying, for a long while.

Little Bean

I dreamt about you last night
You were in my arms
Smiling.

A toothless grin
The happiest creature I have ever seen.
So innocent; so sweet

We were playing in the grass.
It tickled your nose.
And your little toes.

You were in my arms
Smiling.
A toothless grin.

Shimmering, green eyes
Lit up by the sun.

It felt so real.

I did not want to wake.
I wanted to keep this
Precious moment
For as long as I could,

Here I am back in reality

Wishing you were here
With me.

My Sweet Little Bean.

Commute

Driving down the 405. Normal commute time.
Traffic on both sides. North bound. South bound.

80 degrees. During the summertime.

Westchester. Century City. Mullholand Dr.
Los Angeles, City. Streets.

One moment, you're in the beautiful comfort
Of Beverly Hills.

The next, you're on the streets of
Skid Row.

How is that possible?
Driving to a different city. 10 minutes apart.

To witness the difference in living?
The things you see. When stuck in traffic. For
hours.

Everyone has places to be.
But what about the people
On the streets?

Tea

You remembered how
I like my tea.
Earl Grey.
        Splash of milk
        And honey, please.

Nonnie

You would greet us, early in the mornings.
Hugs and kisses.

   WOW, that was bliss.

9 of cups; Full House of hearts.

Nothing, but love you would
Give; Even to those who were
Not of your bloodline.
Strangers. Who became family.
Rewrite our own bloodline.
Homemade meals
With TANG!

DANG, who knew that we wouldn't have that
      Love and luxury from you, again?

Cut up hotdogs with Kraft
Mac and Cheese.
Kool-Aid Jammers juice!
      Cherry please!

NO! Blue Raspberry!
Nap time was the best time
I got to have you
All to myself.
Without anyone else.

While you watched your shows
      As the World Turns
      The Young and the Restless.

I miss going to your house.
And seeing you there.
It's not the same.
Anymore.

I don't visit anymore.

Things changed.

When you physically left this plane.

It's never been the same.

I miss you daily.

We miss you daily

Until we meet again.

My Angel.

Boundaries

D-FENCE!

DEFENSE!

CAUTION YELLOW TAPE!

DO NOT CROSS!

STAY IN YOUR LANE!

I am finally setting boundaries.

Wilmington, DE

Delaware, Wilmington
Gray and dreary.

How I miss the chaos weekday mornings
Silent, sleepy Sundays.

All of Wilmington asleep.
I'm up.

Finally, I can hear you breathe.
A sigh of fresh air.

Get some rest, Wilmington.
As you will need it for the
Monday morning mayhem.

Dead Fish

1 fish
2 fish
Sad fish
Dead fish

Silently weeping
When men would have sex with me
I want this to be over
        Come,
So I can go home.

1 fish
2 fish
Sad fish
Dead fish

So I can cry in the shower
Scrubbing, scraping myself
Of you.
        Come,
So I can go back to normal

1 fish
2 fish
Sad fish
Dead fish

        Come,
So I can pretend like I enjoyed it.

        Come,
So that maybe you will call me back
To do it all over again.

Come,

So that maybe this can be more
than just a hook-up.

1 fish
2 fish
Sad fish
Dead fish

Emotionally, I feel nothing inside
Come,
So I can go home
and Hide my pain.

W.W.W.W.W.H?

Who hurt you?
Who took your power away?
What made you think that it was okay?
When did you realize that it was time for you to take
Back your power?
Where are these thoughts and insecurities rooted from?

> *Childhood traumas?*
> *Family issues?*
> *Relationship problems?*
> *Abandonment?*
> *People pleasing?*

Why do you believe the things about you that aren't True?

Why are you being so hard on yourself?
How can I help you heal?
How can you help yourself heal?
How can I help you remember that you are a beguiling being
Who has so much to offer?
Come with me.

We are going on a journey.
Of healing.
You won't be alone.
> *I Promise.*

Caged

I sit in the house all day
Watching the clouds float by.
The ships of the sky
I run back and forth through the house
It's a maze
Hide and go seek.
I sleep all day; everything feels comfortable
I have everything I want, everything I need.
But, I wonder…
Is there more?
Birds fly without destinations
In sight.
Yet, I'm still here…
In this house…
The door gets left open sometimes.
Now, I could leave and see what the world
Has to offer…
But, I have no desire to leave.
I have everything I want, everything I need.

> *I AM FREE! Right?*
> *Or am I the bird in the cage*
> *That I have created?*

Science

We sat beside each other

In Anatomy.

I wanted to die.

Your touch would send

Electric currents through my body

EKG
STAND BACK!

CLEAR!
ZAP!

Just to keep me alive.

Fuck, dude.

Just let this Chemistry
Die.

Dictionary

I had to look up the
Definition of a word.
Turns out, literally,
Yes, you may fit the description.
The definition.
But in reality,
You don't.
What have you done,
To deserve such a precious title?
What have you done out of the kindness of
Your heart? Without anger?
Without spite?
To deserve such a precious title?

I take the title from you.
Strip it away.

You have to earn it.

Walked outside, 7 AM.
Dense fog. Crows cawing.
Cacophony; alerting one another.
Of the dangers that lurk.
That is near.

I look one dead in the eyes
Silence fills the space.
The air.

What are you doing in my mind?

Messages are what she is trying to send.
Take it all in.
It is now time for you
To access your
Higher Self.

Let us begin,
 My child.

Hot Coffee

I made you coffee
This morning

Pour over;
black
Lately.

*(Used to be with cream until the color looked like
me)*

Sacred Chakra

When you have sex

You don't think about what

Your body absorbs

Physically
Emotionally
Mentally

It's loaded.

You are not a one stop shop
To dump unwanted shit

Sex is beautiful.
Divine.
Sacred.
Sacral Chakra.
Sacred Chakra.

FATHER//DAUGHTER

His eyes would look at me directly.
Dart, like I had a target
On my back.
Ready to attack at any moment
Predator vs. prey.
Every fucking day.

How could you do that?
Knowing you have a daughter?

> *I, too, am*
> *A daughter, of a father.*

How would you feel if a
Father, looked at your
Daughter?
The way you looked at
Me?
How would you feel if a
Father, said the same things
To your
Daughter?
Like you did to
Me?

> *I, too, am*
> *A daughter of a father.*

GOD BLESS AMERICA!

Oh shit! I remember you.
I forgot your name, but not your face.
You're that military dude! I remember you!

GOD BLESS AMERICA!
RED! WHITE! BLUE!

Marine Corp! That's right…
You said that on the site
We met.

GOD BLESS AMERICA!
RED! WHITE! BLUE!

You came all the way up here.
2 hour drive from Camp Pendleton.
Just to put it in,
For 3 minutes.

GOD BLESS AMERICA!
RED! WHITE! BLUE!

Laid up in a Motel 6 room.
Until 11pm.
You went right.
I went left.

GOD BLESS AMERICA!
RED! WHITE! BLUE!

I remember thinking
That was the best
Time I had.
Hopeful, there will be more.

GOD BLESS AMERICA!
RED! WHITE! BLUE!

I waited for a call.
Text from you.
Nothing.

GOD BLESS AMERICA!
RED! WHITE! BLUE!

I remember
I saw a post of yours

GOD BLESS AMERICA!
RED! WHITE! BLUE!

You had your Marine Corp Ball.
I should have known better
Not to fall

GOD BLESS AMERICA!
RED! WHITE! BLUE!

You took someone else.
And that's when I realized
I was nothing but
A booty call

GOD BLESS AMERICA!
RED! WHITE! BLUE!

GOD BLESS THE FREAKS

```
I pledge allegiance
to the flag
of the United States of the Freaks,
and to the Commonwealth
for which it stands,
one society under Goddess,
inseparable,
with freedom for all.
```

GOD BLESS THE FREAKS!
GOD BLESS THE FREAKS!
GOD BLESS THE FREAKS!

SHIT TALK

I knew that people would
Gossip about my family.
About how my mother
Raised us.

5 children.
Hoodlums
Disrespectful
Wild children.

It's the ones closest to you,
That have some out of pocket
Shit to say.
Slinging it with their tongue.

> *I knew monkeys threw shit.*
> *I knew hippos sling shit.*
> *Guess humans do, too.*

20s

20s are a weird age.

You go through everything,
All at once.

And then some
Days, I wish it came with a manual.
A guide,
To prepare me for what I
Am about to go through.

Heartbreaks

Of friends

And lovers

Paths

Of school

Careers

Family

I have begun to understand somethings,
But I know I never fully will.

20s are a weird age.

Robbery

Protect
yourself
at all costs,

even
those
who may
cheer you on

Will
try
to
rob you
of your
happiness.

Uproot and Repot

I get this urge
To up and leave my hometown
To up root
Replant my roots
In a different environment
One that will be beneficial
For my growth
For my development
For my seeds, when They begin to sprout.
To enjoy different climates
That will encourage me
To be a strong plant
And not be dependent on others
Around me.
To not have my energy be dried up
Like that of a well
In a drought
So that I can grow
And my seedlings,
Can sprout.
Repot me.
This space is getting
Smaller.
I'm ready for something
Bigger. Better.
Repot me, in a space Where I can grow
Repot me, so I can be A better person
Lover.
Mother.
Daughter.
Sister.
Repot me.

Semicolon

I have thought about it, you know
Plenty of times.

But I could never bring myself
To it.

I couldn't.
I understand the pain.

You're not alone.
But, hell.

You are so fucking strong.
If it is worth anything,

I love you; I am glad
That you are still here.

MOMMA Pt. 1 - 4

Raised by a woman
Single, Black Woman.
Beautiful, chocolate skin.

Heart of gold
Red lips
Sophisticated.

Heavy her shoulders were,
As she carried the weight of
The world.

To protect one child.
Me.
Mother bear.

Lioness.
A Queen.
Heavy her crown was,

But she wore it with
Ease.
I was raised by a woman.

Single, Black Woman.

II.

Raised by a woman.
Single, Black Woman.
Beautiful, chocolate skin

Heart of gold.
Red lips.
Sophisticated.

Heavy her shoulders were
As she carried the weight of
The world

To protect one child.
Me.
That was until she met, you,

Lifted that weight.
And took it as your own.
With love.

Compassion.
This gave me a father
And four brothers.

Mother bear
Father bear.
A family of 7.

Heavy your crowns were
But, you both wore them with
Ease.

I was raised by a woman and man.
A White Man.
A Black Woman.

III.

Raised by a woman.

Single, Black Woman.
Beautiful, chocolate skin

Heart of gold.
Red lips
Sophisticated.

Heavy her shoulders were
As she carried the weight of
The world.

To protect one child.
Me.
That was until she gained

4 more
Children.
And you got sick.

Nonnie just passed
Which was hard for her.
She lost her mother,

And now,
She's about to lose
You.

From something that was out of
Her control.
Now that you are gone

She has taken on both
Roles.
Mother.
Father.

The weight of the world
And then some…
Has returned to her shoulders.

To protect 5 children,

From the world.

I was raised by a woman.
Single, Black Woman.

IV.

Raised by a woman
Single, Black Woman.
Beautiful, chocolate skin

Heart of gold
Red lips.
Sophisticated.

Heavy her shoulders were
As she carried the weight of
The world.

As she carried the weight of
Pain.
Loss.

Hurt.
Anger.
To protect 5 children.

To protect us.
She would cry, but,
We would never see.

She, too, lost
Herself.
Yet, she kept going.

She had to be strong.
For us.
But, she was tired.

You could see it,
In her eyes.
Yet, she kept going.

Smiling, through it all.
Despite the pain.
Loss.
Hurt.
Anger.

14 years later,
She found ,you,
Accepted her for who
She is.

Accepted her children as
Yours.
You lifted the weight

From her shoulders
With love.
Care.

Gentleness.
And took it as your own.
Selflessness.

This gave me a father.
And 3 brothers.
Mother bear
Father bear.

A family of 10.
Heavy your crowns are
But, you both wear them with
Ease.

I was raised by a woman and
A man.
A Black Woman
A White Man.

Originally, I am a proud product of a Single, Black Woman.

Shadow Play

You stalk me and hide, at
The same time.

    How can you do so?
    You know my deepest darkest
    Secrets.

And celebrate my accomplishments.
You know me better than
I know myself.

I see you in the light,
You disappear in the dark.
Stalker!

    Who are you?

    SHOW YOURSELF!

BRAVO!

The sand is her stage
The moon is her spotlight
The ocean is her orchestra
Oh, what a spectacular night!

Dance, with the waves of the sea.
Under the stars
With me.

She finally freed herself.
Of the pain and suffering.
In her heart.

7.9 billion people
In this world
And
You can still feel
Alone.

WILD THOUGHTS

I lay wide awake
It's still.
Quiet.

                        Except for the racket
                              In my head.
                        There's a riot.

Please leave; I don't want any trouble.
I just want to be left alone.

                              They snort.
                                  Laugh.
                        Continue to rage.
                          If only I could
                Lock them in a fucking cage.
                      I feel like an anchor.
                Being dragged to the bottom
            For I'll never reach the surface
                                   Again.
                      So, why even bother
                  These thoughts have taken
                                    Over.
                        Every inch of me.
                  Sometimes I can shake them
                But, this time it's harder.
                        They come back.
                                  Louder,
                                  LOUDER!

Just leave. I cannot take this.
I beg.
I plead.

            We cannot do that, for the you'll be able
                                  to breathe!

They dance.
        They scream.
Live rent free.
        In my head,
That no longer belongs to me.

I cry.
        And cry.
Begging them to leave.
        They won't.
They have taken over me.
        I have found a way out.
For they won't survive.
        I write this to say.

A farewell and goodbye

Emotionless Object

A being
With
feelings.
Just like
anything
else,

     In this
     chaotic world.

Not
an
object.

     You're worth more than that.
But
you, dear
Have
to
believe
that,

     Yourself.

Joker's Masquerade

Why are you wearing that?

That thing, over your face?

You're covering your expressions.

They don't know that you're suffering?

You, too, are allowed to express.

To feel.

You don't have to always wear

A face of steel.

Who's the fool now?

RAW LOVE

There really aren't any words
To express
the feelings
I have
For you.

Love
can't be explained,
But,
I know it's real.
Raw
Like the honey

from a
Beehive.

Sweet.
It can sting, too.

With disagreements.
Fights.

That's
love.
As long
as your fingers
Are intertwined with
Mine.

Apology

The thought of you doesn't
Anger me.
any more.
Nor am I over the moon.
That's fine,
I allow these emotions to
Come and go
As they please.
I'm glad your doing things
With her
That you never did
With me.
You've grown.
I have too.
People change.
We are supposed to.
Sometimes, a rush of guilt
Does wash up
Here and there.
For the pain and heartache
I put you through,
Was not fair.
I am sorry.
I hurt you.
It won't change,
Nor do I want it to.
Just know,
My heart goes out,
To you.

SNAKE SKIN

The snake
sheds
its skin

Lets go
of what
doesn't serve

You
can shed skin,
too.

CHEERS

I am well know by all
Disliked by some
Loved by most.

I rest upon
Their drunken lips
Night after night

Some ask for me neat,
While others can only have me
Accompanied by something else.

I'm not for everyone.
But I am for some.
They can't get enough of me
The way I smell.
Taste.
The way I look.

Silky, smooth.
how I make them feel.
Classy.
Elegant.

I'm for those
Who
Want to drown their sorrows

I'm for those
Who Need to lose themselves
For the night.

I'm for those
Who
Want to have a good time.

I warm the bodies of those
I come
In contact with.

I warm the throats of those
Who adore me.
Yet, I can be a backstabber.

It burns.
Some nights, I go down,
So smooth, Honey.
Other nights, I won't Stay down.
Even when you try to
Force me too.

You might have had too much
Of me.
I've been there through it all.

Good.
Bad. In Between.
Every sip, I plant a kiss
On your lips. For you to forget
Everything and Nothing.
I am The drug,
You cannot Get enough of it.
I am The drug You cannot
Quit.

BALLOON

I held on too tightly.
It began to cut circulation.
To the strings on my heart.
For the sake of us both,
I needed to let you go.
So that we could float.
In our respective
Directions.

Selfless

Make sure
your cup
Is full,
before
Giving
to others

You can't
give
What you don't have.

Treehouse

I just want to be
In a place, where there are trees.
Where I am at peace.

Blood flows through my veins,
Mimicking the flow of creeks
Running through forests
Mimicking a river's current
Mother Nature's veins.
Together, we are alive.

There's something so magickal
Heavenly, really,
In being
Reminded that there are
Dimensions, realms beyond this world.

Eventually,
You, too, will see with your
Eye, the beauty behind the veil.

Nephews

You make me
remember that
I, too,
have childlike qualities.
Like you.

Painting.
Dancing.
Imagination.

SUGAR OVERLOAD!

Even at 25,
You helped
Keep that part of me
Alive.

Embracing my inner child.
My wild side.

My Grandmother, Willow

Sitting
beneath the trees

Grandmother Willow
whispers

My sweet, divine child,
You are home.

Innocent Boy

Sweet boy,

Who was it

That told you,

Not to express

The rage in your belly?

Love from your heart?

Thoughts that swim,

Aimlessly in your

Mind?

Who was it

That told you,

Not to express

The tears that flow

Like rivers from your

Eye?

Who was it

That told you

Not to express yourself?

Your emotions?

Sweet boy,

Who was it that suppressed

You?

DEATH CARD

What happens when we die?
I like to believe that we go back
To the roots.
Of the world.
Where it all started.
Where we are able to
Rewrite our own truths,
And create new stories.
We don't die,
We simply begin again.

Why are we so afraid of creativity and
Ashamed of Sex?
Sex is art.
Art is creative.
Blending two souls together
To make a
Masterpiece.

CROWN

Creator has a

Reason, for all

Of the events in our life

Whatever it may be

Now is the time to feel whole; complete.

Soul Purpose

Silently sitting, still
Waiting, pondering
What is it that feeds
My soul?

Silently sitting, still
Waiting, pondering
What is it that makes
Me, feel whole?

Silently sitting, still
Waiting, pondering
For something
To fill my bones

Silently sitting, still
Waiting, pondering
While the sun's rays
Softly kiss my cheeks

Leaving behind her lipstick,
Freckles.

Silently sitting, still
Waiting, pondering
While winds whisper
Sweet nothings

Pieces of grass
Tickle the tips
Of my toes.

Silently sitting, still
Waiting, pondering
While clouds pass by
Shape shifting

Silently sitting, still
Waiting, pondering
Coming to conclusion
That this is life

Beautiful, blissful life
Is what feeds
My soul
Is what makes me

Whole. As I go
Through this life,
I transform

Like butterflies
Finally finding
My soul's purpose.

On this realm.
On this plane.
On this Earth.
In this moment.

Silently sitting, still
Embracing, loving
Myself.
My soul.

Wholeheartedly.
Unconditionally.

I know
My purpose.

Printed in Poland
by Amazon Fulfillment
Poland Sp. z o.o., Wrocław
09 May 2022

7b3d7b3c-54a8-4b0a-82b7-59ea9e00746fR01